Artificial Intelligence:

A Beginner's Guide to Understanding and Implementing AI

By Oluchi Ike

Table of Contents

Introduction:

- Definition of AI

- Brief overview of AI's evolution

- Importance and impact of AI in modern society

- Outline of what will be covered in the book

Chapter 1: The History of Artificial Intelligence

- Early concepts and origins of AI

- Key milestones in AI development

- Important figures in AI history

- Evolution from early AI to modern AI

Chapter 2: Key Concepts and Terminology

- Definition of key terms (AI, machine learning, deep learning, etc.)

- Explanation of fundamental AI concepts

- Different types of AI (narrow AI, general AI, superintelligent AI)

Chapter 3: Machine Learning and Deep Learning

- Explanation of machine learning

- Types of machine learning (supervised, unsupervised, reinforcement)

- Introduction to deep learning

- Neural networks and how they work

Chapter 4: Natural Language Processing

- What is Natural Language Processing (NLP)?

- Applications of NLP (chatbots, language translation, sentiment analysis)

- Key techniques used in NLP

Chapter 5: Computer Vision

- What is computer vision?

- Applications of computer vision (image recognition, autonomous vehicles)

- Techniques and technologies in computer vision

Chapter 6: AI in Healthcare

- Overview of AI applications in healthcare
- Case studies (e.g., AI in diagnostics, personalized medicine)
- Benefits and challenges of AI in healthcare

Chapter 7: AI in Business

- Overview of AI applications in business
- Case studies (e.g., AI in marketing, supply chain management)
- Benefits and challenges of AI in business

Chapter 8: Ethical Considerations in AI

- Ethical issues related to AI (bias, privacy, job displacement)
- The importance of ethical AI development
- Strategies for addressing ethical challenges in AI

Chapter 9: Future Trends in AI

- Emerging trends and technologies in AI

- Predictions for the future of AI

- How AI might shape various industries in the future

Conclusion:

- Recap of the key points covered in the book

- Final thoughts on the importance of understanding and responsibly implementing AI

Summary in Layman's Terms:

- Simplified summary of the key concepts and takeaways from the book

- Easy-to-understand explanations for readers without a technical background

---

Glossary:

- Definitions of key terms and concepts used throughout the book

---

Case Studies:

- Detailed case studies of successful AI implementations in various industries
- Lessons learned and best practices from these case studies

References:

- List of sources and additional reading materials for readers who want to delve deeper into AI

Preface

Welcome to ***Artificial Intelligence: A Beginner's Guide to Understanding and Implementing AI***. The rapid development of AI technology has transformed many aspects of our lives, from how we communicate to how we work and play. This book is designed to demystify AI, making it accessible to anyone with an interest in the subject. Whether you are a student, a professional looking to integrate AI into your business, or simply a curious reader, this guide will provide you with a comprehensive understanding of AI, its applications, and its implications for the future. We hope you find this book both informative and inspiring as you embark on your journey into the fascinating world of artificial intelligence.

A serene image of a person reading a book about AI, with a holographic representation of artificial intelligence concepts floating above the book

Foreword

Artificial Intelligence (AI) is no longer a futuristic concept confined to the realm of science fiction; it is a transformative force reshaping industries, economies, and our daily lives. As someone who has been deeply involved in the AI field for over two decades, I have witnessed its evolution from a theoretical discipline to a practical and essential technology.

This book, ***Artificial Intelligence: A Beginner's Guide to Understanding and Implementing AI****, arrives at a pivotal moment. AI is rapidly becoming an integral part of our world, and understanding its potential and limitations is crucial for everyone. Whether you're a business leader aiming to leverage AI for competitive advantage, a student aspiring to enter the tech industry, or a curious individual eager to understand how AI impacts your life, this book offers valuable insights.

The author has done a commendable job of breaking down complex concepts into digestible pieces, making AI accessible to a broad audience. The blend of historical context, technical explanation, real-world applications, and ethical considerations provides a well-rounded introduction to AI.

I am excited to see how this book will contribute to spreading knowledge about AI and inspiring future innovations. As you read through these pages, I hope you will gain not only an understanding of AI but also an appreciation for its potential to drive positive change in our world.

Warm regards,

Image of a group of diverse professionals engaged in a discussion around a table, with AI-related icons and symbols (like neural networks, robots, data steams) overlayed around them

Introduction

Artificial Intelligence (AI) is one of the most exciting and rapidly evolving fields in technology today. From self-driving cars and virtual assistants to personalized recommendations and advanced medical diagnostics, AI is revolutionizing how we live and work. But what exactly is AI, and how does it work?

This book is designed to be your comprehensive guide to understanding AI. We will start by exploring the history of AI, tracing its development from early theoretical concepts to the advanced technologies we have today. We'll then dive into the key concepts and terminology you'll need to grasp the fundamentals of AI.

You will learn about machine learning and deep learning, two critical components of AI that enable machines to learn from data and make decisions. We'll also explore natural language processing and computer vision, two exciting areas of AI that allow machines to understand and interact with the world in ways that were once the exclusive domain of humans.

In addition to these technical topics, we will look at the practical applications of AI in various industries, including healthcare and business. You will read case studies that highlight how AI is being used to solve real-world problems and drive innovation.

Ethical considerations are also a crucial part of the AI discussion. As AI continues to advance, it raises important questions about privacy, bias, and the future of work. We will examine these issues and discuss strategies for developing and implementing AI responsibly.

Finally, we will look ahead to the future of AI, exploring emerging trends and potential developments. The book concludes with a summary of key points in layman's terms, a glossary of terms, and detailed case studies to reinforce your understanding.

Whether you're new to AI or looking to deepen your knowledge, this book will provide you with the insights and information you need to navigate the world of AI. Let's embark on this journey together and discover the incredible possibilities of artificial intelligence.

A futuristic cityscape showing various AI applications like self-driving cars, drones, and digital billboards with AI advertisements

A timeline of AI development with key milestones and famous figures in AI history, featuring early computers, Turing, McCarthy, and modern AI robots

Chapter 1

The History of Artificial Intelligence

Artificial Intelligence has a rich and fascinating history that spans several decades. Understanding this history is crucial to appreciate how far we've come and where we're headed.

Early Concepts and Origins of AI

The concept of machines that can think and learn dates back to ancient mythology and philosophy. However, the formal study of AI began in the 20th century. In 1950, British mathematician and logician Alan Turing published a landmark paper titled "Computing Machinery and Intelligence," which posed the question, "Can machines think?" Turing proposed the famous Turing Test, a method for determining whether a machine exhibits intelligent behavior indistinguishable from that of a human.

Key Milestones in AI Development

The term "Artificial Intelligence" was coined in 1956 during the Dartmouth Conference, organized by John McCarthy, Marvin Minsky, Nathaniel Rochester, and Claude Shannon. This event marked the birth of AI as a field of study. The early years of AI research were marked by optimism and ambitious projects, such as the General Problem Solver (GPS) developed by Allen Newell and Herbert A. Simon.

Important Figures in AI History

Several pioneers have made significant contributions to AI. Alan Turing's work laid the foundation for AI research. John McCarthy, often called the "Father of AI," developed the Lisp programming language, which became essential for AI development. Marvin Minsky's work in cognitive psychology and robotics also played a crucial role.

Evolution from Early AI to Modern AI

The initial excitement about AI led to the development of early AI programs that could solve algebra problems, prove theorems, and play games like chess. However, progress slowed in the 1970s and 1980s due to limitations in computing power and over-ambitious goals, a period known as the "AI winter."

The resurgence of AI in the 21st century can be attributed to several factors, including the advent of powerful computers, the availability of vast amounts of data, and breakthroughs in machine learning algorithms. Today, AI is an integral part of our technology landscape, driving innovations in various fields.

A visual representation of key AI concepts and terms like machine learning, neural networks, and natural language processing, interconnected by data streams

Chapter 2

Key Concepts and Terminology

Artificial Intelligence (AI) is a broad and complex field with its own set of terms and concepts. Understanding these basics is essential for grasping the more advanced topics we'll cover later. This chapter will define key terms and explain fundamental concepts in AI.

Definition of Key Terms

Artificial Intelligence (AI)

The simulation of human intelligence in machines that are programmed to think and learn. AI can perform tasks that typically require human intelligence, such as visual perception, speech recognition, decision-making, and language translation.

Machine Learning (ML)

A subset of AI that involves training algorithms to learn from and make predictions or decisions based on data. ML algorithms improve their performance over time as they are exposed to more data.

Deep Learning (DL)

A subset of machine learning that uses neural networks with many layers (deep neural networks) to model complex patterns in data. It is particularly effective in tasks such as image and speech recognition.

Neural Networks

Computational models inspired by the human brain, consisting of interconnected nodes (neurons) that process data in layers. Neural networks are the backbone of deep learning.

Natural Language Processing (NLP)

A branch of AI focused on the interaction between computers and humans through natural language. NLP enables machines to understand, interpret, and respond to human language.

Computer Vision

An area of AI that enables machines to interpret and make decisions based on visual data from the world, such as images and videos.

Explanation of Fundamental AI Concepts

Algorithms

Step-by-step procedures or formulas for solving problems. In AI, algorithms process data to generate predictions, decisions, or other outputs.

Training Data

The dataset used to train an AI model. Training data must be representative of the real-world scenarios the AI will encounter to ensure accurate and reliable performance.

Model

The output of the training process. A model represents the learned patterns from the training data and can be used to make predictions or decisions.

Supervised Learning

A type of machine learning where the model is trained on labeled data, meaning each training example includes the correct output. The model learns to map inputs to outputs.

Unsupervised Learning

A type of machine learning where the model is trained on unlabeled data. The model tries to learn the underlying patterns or structures in the data without explicit instructions on what to predict.

Reinforcement Learning

A type of machine learning where an agent learns to make decisions by receiving rewards or penalties for its actions. The goal is to maximize cumulative rewards.

Different Types of AI

Narrow AI (Weak AI)

AI systems designed to perform a specific task or a narrow set of tasks. Examples include voice assistants like Siri and Alexa, which are proficient in specific functions but lack general intelligence.

General AI (Strong AI)

Hypothetical AI systems that possess the ability to perform any intellectual task that a human can do. General AI does not yet exist and remains a topic of research and speculation.

Superintelligent AI

A theoretical form of AI that surpasses human intelligence in all aspects, including creativity, problem-solving, and social intelligence. The concept of superintelligent AI raises significant ethical and existential questions.

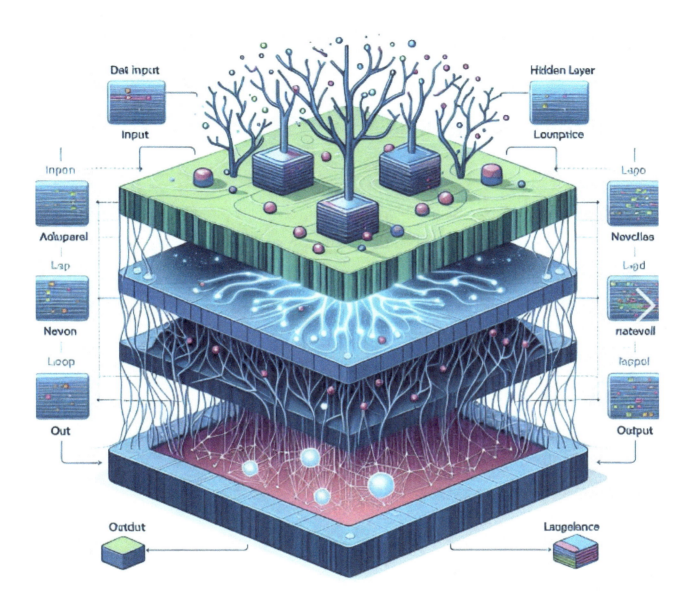

An illustration of a neural network in action, showing data input, hidden layers with neurons, and output with labeled results

Chapter 3

Machine Learning and Deep Learning

Machine learning (ML) and deep learning (DL) are core components of modern AI. This chapter will explain these concepts, their types, and how they work.

Explanation of Machine Learning

Machine learning involves training algorithms to recognize patterns in data and make predictions or decisions without being explicitly programmed for each task. ML can be broadly categorized into three types:

1. Supervised Learning:

- **Definition**: The model is trained on labeled data, meaning each training example includes the correct output.
- **Example**: Email spam detection, where the algorithm learns to classify emails as spam or not based on labeled examples.

2. Unsupervised Learning:

- **Definition**: The model is trained on unlabeled data, meaning the algorithm tries to find patterns or structures in the data without explicit instructions on what to predict.
- **Example**: Customer segmentation, where the algorithm groups customers based on purchasing behavior without predefined labels.

3. Reinforcement Learning:

- **Definition**: An agent learns to make decisions by receiving rewards or penalties for its actions. The goal is to maximize cumulative rewards.
- **Example**: Game playing, where the algorithm learns to play games like chess or Go by receiving rewards for winning and penalties for losing.

Introduction to Deep Learning

Deep learning is a subset of machine learning that uses neural networks with many layers to model complex patterns in data. It has achieved significant breakthroughs in areas such as image and speech recognition.

Neural Networks and How They Work

Neural networks are inspired by the structure and function of the human brain. They consist of layers of interconnected nodes (neurons) that process data.

- Layers of Neural Networks:

- o **Input Layer**: Receives the input data.
- o **Hidden Layers**: Process the input data through multiple layers of neurons.
- o **Output Layer**: Produces the final output based on the processed data.

- Training Neural Networks:

- o **Forward Propagation**: Data passes through the network from the input layer to the output layer, generating predictions.
- o **Backward Propagation**: The network adjusts its weights based on the difference between predicted and actual outcomes, improving accuracy over time.

Applications of Deep Learning

Deep learning has enabled significant advancements in various fields, including:

- o **Image Recognition**: Used in facial recognition systems and medical image analysis.
- o **Speech Recognition**: Powers virtual assistants like Siri and Google Assistant.
- o **Natural Language Processing**: Enables language translation, sentiment analysis, and chatbots.

An AI-powered chatbot interacting with a human, with text bubbles and speech waves indicating natural language processing

Chapter 4

Natural Language Processing

Natural Language Processing (NLP) is a critical area of AI that focuses on the interaction between computers and humans through natural language. This chapter will delve into NLP, its applications, and key techniques.

What is Natural Language Processing (NLP)?

NLP enables machines to understand, interpret, and respond to human language. It combines linguistics, computer science, and AI to bridge the gap between human communication and machine understanding.

Applications of NLP

- o **Chatbots**: Automated programs that interact with users through text or voice, providing customer service or answering queries.
- o **Language Translation**: Systems like Google Translate that convert text from one language to another.
- o **Sentiment Analysis**: Tools that analyze text to determine the sentiment behind it, often used in social media monitoring.

Key Techniques Used in NLP

- **Tokenization**: Breaking down text into smaller units, such as words or sentences, to analyze them more easily.

- **Part-of-Speech Tagging**: Identifying the grammatical parts of speech (nouns, verbs, adjectives, etc.) in a sentence.

- **Named Entity Recognition (NER):** Identifying and classifying entities (names, dates, locations) in text.

- **Parsing:** Analyzing the grammatical structure of a sentence to understand its meaning.

- **Machine Translation**: Using algorithms to translate text from one language to another.

- **Text Classification**: Categorizing text into predefined categories, such as spam detection or topic labeling.

A computer's view of the world, identifying objects like people, cars, and trees with bounding boxes and labels

Chapter 5

Computer Vision

Computer Vision is a fascinating field within AI that enables machines to interpret and make decisions based on visual data from the world. This chapter will explore the basics of computer vision, its applications, and the techniques used in this area.

What is Computer Vision?

Computer Vision is the process of using algorithms to interpret and understand images and videos. It involves the automatic extraction, analysis, and understanding of useful information from a single image or a sequence of images.

Applications of Computer Vision

- **Image Recognition**: Identifying objects, people, or features in images. Used in security systems, social media tagging, and medical diagnostics.
- **Autonomous Vehicles**: Enabling self-driving cars to recognize and respond to their environment, including road signs, pedestrians, and other vehicles.
- **Facial Recognition**: Detecting and verifying individuals based on their facial features. Used in security, authentication, and personalization.
- **Augmented Reality (AR):** Overlaying digital information on the real world, as seen in applications like Pokémon Go and various AR shopping experiences.
- **Healthcare**: Analyzing medical images, such as X-rays and MRIs, to detect diseases and conditions.

Techniques and Technologies in Computer Vision

- **Image Processing**: Manipulating and transforming images to enhance them or extract useful information. Techniques include filtering, edge detection, and image segmentation.

- **Feature Extraction**: Identifying and extracting important features from images, such as edges, textures, and shapes, to analyze and classify objects.

- **Object Detection**: Locating and identifying objects within an image. Techniques like YOLO (You Only Look Once) and R-CNN (Region-based Convolutional Neural Networks) are commonly used.

- **Convolutional Neural Networks (CNNs):** A type of deep learning model specifically designed for processing structured grid data like images. CNNs are highly effective in image recognition and classification tasks.

- **Optical Character Recognition (OCR):** Converting different types of documents, such as scanned paper documents, PDFs, or images captured by a digital camera, into editable and searchable data.

Challenges in Computer Vision

- o **Variability in Images**: Differences in lighting, angle, and occlusion can make it difficult for algorithms to accurately interpret images.
- o **Real-time Processing**: For applications like autonomous vehicles, processing visual data in real-time is crucial but computationally intensive.
- o **Data Quality and Quantity**: High-quality, annotated datasets are essential for training accurate computer vision models. Collecting and annotating such data can be challenging and time-consuming.

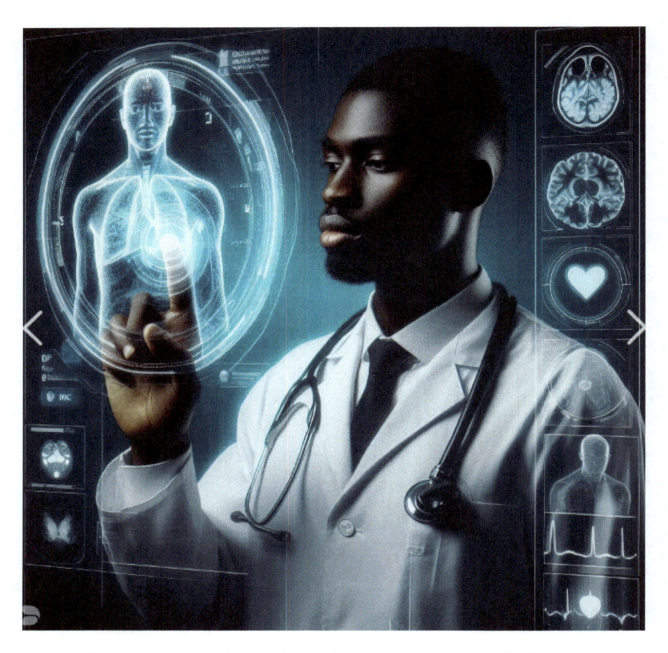

A doctor using an AI-powered device to analyze medical images, with a holographic display showing diagnostic results

Chapter 6

AI in Healthcare

Artificial Intelligence has immense potential to transform the healthcare industry. This chapter will examine the applications of AI in healthcare, highlighting its benefits and challenges through case studies.

Overview of AI Applications in Healthcare

AI is being used to enhance various aspects of healthcare, from diagnostics and treatment to patient care and administration. Here are some key applications:

- **Medical Imaging**: AI algorithms analyze medical images (X-rays, MRIs, CT scans) to detect abnormalities such as tumors, fractures, and infections. This can lead to faster and more accurate diagnoses.
- **Personalized Medicine**: AI helps in tailoring treatments to individual patients based on their genetic makeup, lifestyle, and other factors, leading to more effective and targeted therapies.
- **Predictive Analytics**: AI models predict disease outbreaks, patient readmissions, and treatment outcomes, enabling proactive and preventive healthcare measures.
- **Virtual Health Assistants**: AI-powered chatbots and virtual assistants provide patients with medical information, symptom checks, and appointment scheduling, improving accessibility and convenience.
- **Drug Discovery**: AI accelerates the drug discovery process by analyzing vast amounts of data to identify potential drug candidates and predict their effectiveness.

Case Studies

1. AI in Radiology:

- ○ **Application**: AI algorithms assist radiologists in interpreting medical images, highlighting areas of concern that may require further examination.
- ○ **Benefit**: Reduces the workload of radiologists, improves accuracy in diagnosis, and expedites the diagnostic process.
- ○ **Example**: Google Health's AI system for detecting breast cancer in mammograms has shown to be as accurate as human radiologists.

2. AI in Personalized Medicine:

- ○ **Application**: AI analyzes patient data to recommend personalized treatment plans.
- ○ **Benefit**: Increases the effectiveness of treatments and reduces adverse reactions.
- ○ **Example**: IBM Watson for Oncology uses AI to provide oncologists with evidence-based treatment options tailored to individual patients.

3. AI in Predictive Analytics:

- o **Application**: Predictive models analyze patient data to foresee health events, such as the likelihood of readmission or disease progression.
- o **Benefit**: Allows for early intervention and preventive measures, improving patient outcomes.
- o **Example**: Hospitals use AI to predict patient readmissions, enabling better discharge planning and follow-up care.

Benefits and Challenges of AI in Healthcare

- Benefits:

- o Improved diagnostic accuracy
- o Faster and more efficient healthcare delivery
- o Personalized treatment options
- o Enhanced patient engagement and satisfaction

- Challenges:

- o Data privacy and security concerns
- o Need for high-quality, annotated data
- o Integration with existing healthcare systems
- o Ethical considerations and regulatory compliance

A business meeting with AI-driven analytics displayed on a large screen, showing graphs and insights derived from data

Chapter 7

AI in Business

Artificial Intelligence is revolutionizing the business world by driving efficiency, enhancing customer experiences, and enabling data-driven decision-making. This chapter explores the various applications of AI in business, illustrated through case studies.

Overview of AI Applications in

Business

AI is being used across multiple business functions, including marketing, finance, supply chain, and customer service. Here are some key applications:

- o **Marketing and Sales**: AI analyzes customer data to provide personalized recommendations, predict customer behavior, and optimize marketing campaigns. Chatbots and virtual assistants enhance customer engagement.
- o **Finance and Accounting**: AI automates routine tasks such as data entry and fraud detection, and provides predictive analytics for investment decisions and risk management.
- o **Supply Chain Management**: AI optimizes supply chain operations by predicting demand, managing inventory, and improving logistics.
- o **Human Resources**: AI assists in talent acquisition by screening resumes, analyzing candidate profiles, and predicting employee performance and retention.
- o **Customer Service**: AI-powered chatbots and virtual assistants provide 24/7 customer support, resolving queries and issues efficiently.

Case Studies

1. AI in Marketing and Sales:

- **Application**: Personalized product recommendations based on customer behavior and preferences.
- **Benefit**: Increases customer engagement and sales conversion rates.
- **Example**: Amazon's recommendation engine, which accounts for a significant percentage of sales by suggesting products to customers based on their browsing and purchasing history.

2. AI in Finance:

- **Application**: Fraud detection through pattern recognition and anomaly detection.
- **Benefit**: Reduces financial losses due to fraudulent activities and improves security.
- **Example**: PayPal uses AI to detect and prevent fraudulent transactions, enhancing trust and security for its users.

3. AI in Supply Chain Management:

- o **Application**: Demand forecasting to optimize inventory levels and reduce waste.
- o **Benefit**: Improves efficiency and reduces costs by ensuring that products are available when needed without overstocking.
- o **Example**: Walmart uses AI to predict demand for various products, ensuring optimal inventory management and reducing stockouts.

Benefits and Challenges of AI in Business

- Benefits:

- o Increased operational efficiency
- o Enhanced customer experiences
- o Data-driven decision-making
- o Cost reduction and resource optimization

- Challenges:

- o Data privacy and security concerns
- o Integration with existing systems and processes
- o Need for skilled personnel to develop and manage AI systems
- o Ethical considerations and regulatory compliance

A balanced scale with AI icons on one side and symbols representing ethics, fairness, and privacy on the other

Chapter 8

Ethical Considerations in AI

The rapid advancement of AI technology has raised significant ethical questions and challenges. This chapter explores these ethical considerations, the importance of developing ethical AI, and strategies for addressing these challenges.

Ethical Issues Related to AI

- Bias and Fairness:

- o **Problem**: AI systems can inherit biases present in the training data, leading to unfair and discriminatory outcomes.
- o **Example**: Facial recognition systems that perform poorly on certain racial or ethnic groups due to biased training data.
- o **Solution**: Use diverse and representative datasets, implement fairness-aware algorithms, and regularly audit AI systems for bias.

- Privacy:

- o **Problem**: AI systems often rely on large amounts of personal data, raising concerns about data privacy and security.
- o **Example**: AI-driven advertising platforms that collect and analyze user data without explicit consent.
- o **Solution**: Implement robust data protection measures, ensure transparency in data usage, and comply with privacy regulations like GDPR.

- Job Displacement:

- o **Problem**: AI and automation can lead to job losses in certain sectors, affecting workers and communities.
- o **Example**: The automation of manufacturing jobs leading to layoffs and economic disruption.
- o **Solution**: Promote reskilling and upskilling programs, create new job opportunities in emerging fields, and develop policies to support affected workers.

The Importance of Ethical AI Development

Ethical AI development is crucial for several reasons:

- o **Trust and Acceptance**: Ensuring that AI systems are fair, transparent, and accountable builds public trust and acceptance of AI technology.
- o **Legal and Regulatory Compliance**: Adhering to ethical guidelines and regulations helps avoid legal issues and fosters responsible AI development.
- o **Social Responsibility**: Ethical AI development aligns with broader societal values and promotes the well-being of individuals and communities.

Strategies for Addressing Ethical Challenges in AI

1. Transparency:

- o Make AI systems transparent by providing clear explanations of how they work and the decision-making processes involved.
- o Example: Explainable AI (XAI) techniques that make AI models more interpretable and understandable.

2. Accountability:

- o Establish clear lines of accountability for AI systems, ensuring that developers and organizations are responsible for their AI's outcomes.
- o Example: Implementing robust governance frameworks and ethical guidelines for AI development and deployment.

3. Inclusivity:

- o Involve diverse stakeholders in the AI development process to ensure that different perspectives and values are considered.
- o Example: Engaging ethicists, social scientists, and community representatives in AI project teams.

4. Continuous Monitoring and Evaluation:

- o Regularly monitor and evaluate AI systems to identify and mitigate any ethical issues that arise.
- o Example: Conducting periodic audits and assessments of AI systems to ensure they remain fair, transparent, and accountable.

Case Studies

1. AI Bias in Hiring:

- o **Issue**: An AI-powered hiring tool was found to be biased against female candidates due to biased training data.
- o **Action**: The company revised the training data and implemented fairness-aware algorithms to reduce bias.
- o **Outcome**: Improved fairness in hiring decisions and increased diversity in the workforce.

2. AI and Data Privacy:

- o **Issue**: A social media platform faced backlash for using AI to analyze user data without consent.
- o **Action**: The platform updated its privacy policies, implemented stronger data protection measures, and provided users with more control over their data.
- o **Outcome**: Enhanced user trust and compliance with data privacy regulations.

3. Job Displacement Due to AI:

- o **Issue**: Automation led to significant job losses in a manufacturing sector.

- o **Action**: The affected company invested in reskilling programs for displaced workers and collaborated with local governments to create new job opportunities in emerging industries.

- o **Outcome**: Successful transition of workers to new roles and reduced economic disruption.

A futuristic laboratory with AI researchers working on advanced AI technologies like quantum computing and edge computing

Chapter 9

Future Trends in AI

Artificial Intelligence continues to evolve, and its future holds immense possibilities. This chapter explores emerging trends and potential developments in AI that could shape various industries and aspects of our lives.

Emerging Trends in AI

1. AI and Quantum Computing:

- **Description**: Quantum computing has the potential to revolutionize AI by providing unprecedented computational power. This could lead to significant advancements in AI capabilities, including solving complex problems that are currently intractable.
- **Example**: Quantum machine learning algorithms that can process vast amounts of data more efficiently than classical algorithms.

2. AI and Edge Computing:

- **Description**: Edge computing involves processing data closer to its source rather than relying on centralized cloud servers. This trend is crucial for AI applications that require real-time processing and low latency.
- **Example**: AI-powered IoT devices that can make instant decisions based on local data, such as autonomous drones and smart home systems.

3. AI and Explainability:

- o **Description**: As AI systems become more complex, there is a growing emphasis on making them explainable and interpretable. Explainable AI (XAI) aims to provide clear and understandable explanations of AI decisions.
- o **Example**: AI models in healthcare that provide doctors with transparent explanations of their diagnostic recommendations.

4. AI and Ethical AI Development:

- o **Description**: The focus on ethical AI development is expected to intensify, with increased efforts to address bias, fairness, and accountability. This trend will shape AI policies, regulations, and best practices.
- o **Example**: Development of international ethical guidelines for AI and increased collaboration between governments, organizations, and academia.

Predictions for the Future of AI

1. AI in Everyday Life:

- o AI will become increasingly integrated into our daily lives, from smart personal assistants and autonomous vehicles to intelligent home appliances and wearable health monitors.

2. AI in Healthcare:

- o AI will continue to advance medical diagnostics, personalized medicine, and treatment planning, leading to improved patient outcomes and reduced healthcare costs.

3. AI in Business and Industry:

- o AI will drive further automation and optimization of business processes, leading to increased efficiency, innovation, and competitive advantage.

4. AI in Education:

- o AI will transform education by providing personalized learning experiences, intelligent tutoring systems, and advanced educational tools.

5. AI and the Workforce:

- o AI will reshape the workforce, with new job roles emerging in AI development, maintenance, and oversight, while some traditional roles may become obsolete. Reskilling and upskilling will be essential.

How AI Might Shape Various Industries in the Future

1. Healthcare:

- AI will enable early disease detection, precision medicine, and advanced telehealth services, improving access to quality healthcare worldwide.

2. Finance:

- AI will enhance fraud detection, risk management, and investment strategies, making financial services more secure and efficient.

3. Retail:

- AI will revolutionize retail by providing personalized shopping experiences, optimizing supply chains, and enhancing customer service.

4. Transportation:

- AI will drive the development of autonomous vehicles, smart traffic management systems, and efficient logistics networks, reducing congestion and emissions.

5. Energy:

- AI will optimize energy consumption, improve grid management, and accelerate the transition to renewable energy sources, contributing to a sustainable future.

A vision of a bright future where AI is integrated seamlessly into daily life, enhancing human capabilities and fostering innovation

Conclusion

As we've explored throughout this book, Artificial Intelligence holds tremendous potential to transform various aspects of our lives and industries. From its historical development to the

cutting-edge technologies of today, AI is a field that continues to evolve rapidly.

Understanding AI's key concepts, applications, and ethical considerations is essential for leveraging its benefits while addressing its challenges. By promoting ethical AI development and staying informed about emerging trends, we can harness AI's power to drive positive change and innovation.

Thank you for joining us on this journey through the fascinating world of AI. We hope this book has provided you with valuable insights and a deeper appreciation for the transformative potential of artificial intelligence.

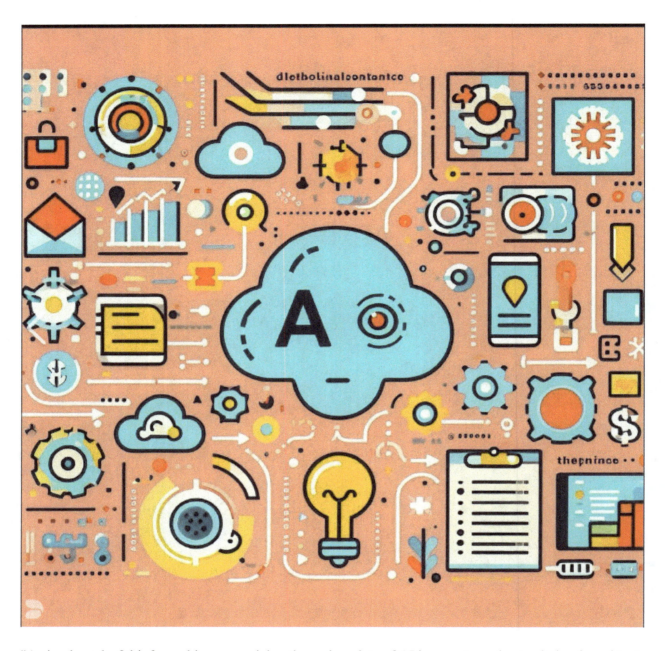

"A simple, colorful infographic summarizing the main points of AI in easy-to-understand visuals and text

Summary in Layman's Terms

Artificial Intelligence (AI) is revolutionizing our world, but understanding it doesn't have to be complicated. Here's a simplified summary of the key points from this book.

What is AI?

AI is the creation of machines that can think and learn like humans. These machines can perform tasks that typically require human intelligence, such as recognizing faces, understanding language, and making decisions.

Key Concepts

- **Machine Learning (ML):** A method where machines learn from data to make decisions or predictions without being explicitly programmed for each task. It's like teaching a computer by showing it many examples.

- **Deep Learning (DL):** A type of machine learning that uses neural networks with many layers to analyze data. It's especially good at recognizing images and understanding speech.

- **Neural Networks:** These are computer systems inspired by the human brain. They consist of interconnected nodes (neurons) that process information in layers.

- **Natural Language Processing (NLP):** This allows machines to understand and respond to human language. Think of chatbots and virtual assistants like Siri or Alexa.

- **Computer Vision:** The technology that enables machines to interpret and make decisions based on visual data, like recognizing objects in photos or videos.

Applications of AI

- **Healthcare**: AI helps doctors diagnose diseases from medical images, predict patient outcomes, and personalize treatments.

- **Business**: Companies use AI to improve customer service with chatbots, personalize marketing, manage supply chains, and detect fraud.

- **Everyday Life**: AI powers the recommendations you get on Netflix, the voice assistants on your phone, and even the systems in self-driving cars.

Ethical Considerations

- **Bias**: AI can sometimes be unfair if it learns from biased data. It's important to use diverse and representative data to avoid discrimination.

- **Privacy**: AI systems often use personal data, which raises concerns about how that data is protected and used.

- **Job Displacement**: As AI automates tasks, some jobs may be lost. However, new jobs in AI development and maintenance will also be created. Reskilling workers is crucial.

Future Trends

- **Quantum Computing**: This could provide the computational power to solve complex AI problems much faster.

- **Edge Computing**: Processing data closer to where it's collected, which is important for real-time applications like autonomous vehicles.

- **Explainable AI**: Making AI systems transparent and understandable so people can trust and manage them better.

- **Ethical AI Development**: Increasing focus on developing AI responsibly, addressing bias, privacy, and job displacement.

Conclusion

AI is a powerful tool that's transforming various aspects of our lives. Understanding its basic concepts, applications, and ethical considerations helps us use it wisely and prepare for its future developments. By promoting ethical AI development and staying informed about emerging trends, we can harness AI's potential for positive change and innovation.

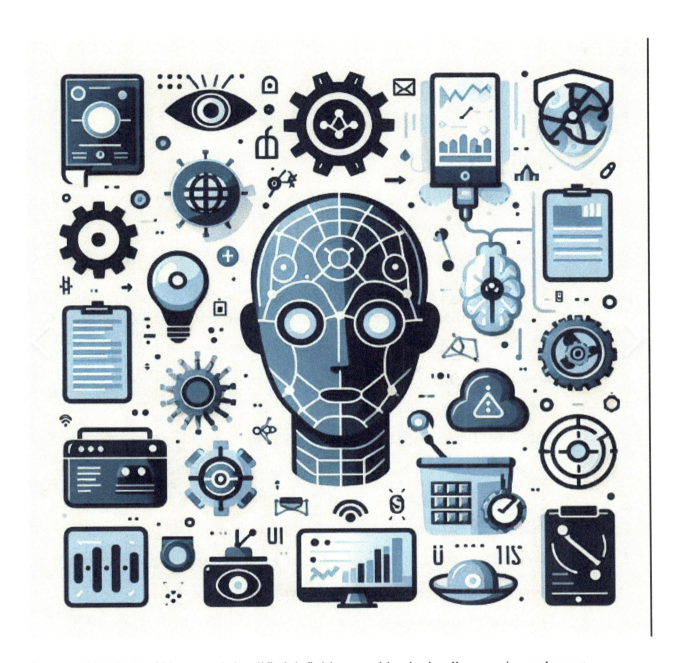

A page with AI-related icons and simplified definitions, making it visually engaging and easy to understand

Glossary

- **Algorithm**: A step-by-step procedure for solving a problem or performing a task.
- **Artificial Intelligence (AI):** The simulation of human intelligence in machines that can think and learn.
- **Bias**: A prejudice in favor or against something that can affect the fairness of AI decisions.
- **Computer Vision**: A field of AI that enables machines to interpret and understand visual information from the world.
- **Deep Learning (DL):** A type of machine learning that uses neural networks with many layers to analyze data.
- **Machine Learning (ML):** A method where machines learn from data to make decisions or predictions without being explicitly programmed.
- **Natural Language Processing (NLP):** The ability of machines to understand and interact with human language.
- **Neural Networks:** Computer systems inspired by the human brain that process information in interconnected nodes (neurons).
- **Quantum Computing**: A type of computing that uses quantum-mechanical phenomena to perform operations on data at incredibly fast speeds.
- **Reinforcement Learning**: A type of machine learning where an agent learns to make decisions by receiving rewards or penalties for its actions.
- **Supervised Learning**: A type of machine learning where the model is trained on labeled data.

- **Unsupervised Learning**: A type of machine learning where the model is trained on unlabeled data to find patterns or structures.

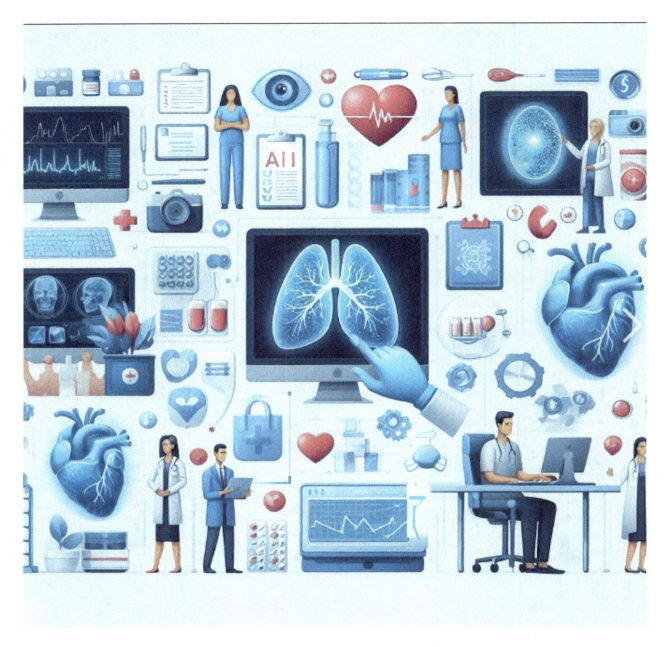

Illustrative images for each case study, such as an AI system analyzing medical images, personalized medicine, and an AI-driven marketing campaign

Case Studies

Case Study 1: AI in Radiology

Issue: Radiologists face a high workload and risk of missing critical diagnoses.

Action: An AI algorithm was developed to assist in interpreting medical images, highlighting areas of concern.

Outcome: Reduced workload for radiologists, improved accuracy in diagnoses, and faster diagnostic processes. Google Health's AI system for detecting breast cancer in mammograms demonstrated accuracy comparable to human radiologists.

Case Study 2: AI in Personalized Medicine

Issue: Generic treatments may not be effective for all patients.

Action: IBM Watson for Oncology uses AI to analyze patient data and provide oncologists with personalized treatment options based on individual patient profiles.

Outcome: Increased effectiveness of treatments and reduced adverse reactions, leading to better patient outcomes.

Case Study 3: AI in Marketing and Sales

Issue: Businesses need to engage customers and increase sales conversion rates.

Action: Amazon's recommendation engine uses AI to suggest products based on customer behavior and preferences.

Outcome: Significant increase in customer engagement and sales, with product recommendations accounting for a substantial percentage of Amazon's sales.

References

1. Turing, A. M. (1950). Computing Machinery and Intelligence. Mind, 59, 433-460.

2. McCarthy, J., Minsky, M., Rochester, N., & Shannon, C. E. (1956). A Proposal for the Dartmouth Summer Research Project on Artificial Intelligence.

3. LeCun, Y., Bengio, Y., & Hinton, G. (2015). Deep Learning. Nature, 521, 436-444.

4. Goodfellow, I., Bengio, Y., & Courville, A. (2016). Deep Learning. MIT Press.

5. Russell, S., & Norvig, P. (2010). Artificial Intelligence: A Modern Approach (3rd ed.). Prentice Hall.

Note -

The End